Walt Disney World & Florida Keys Travel Guide

Attractions, Eating, Drinking, Shopping & Places To Stay

Adam Holt

Copyright © 2014, Astute Press
All Rights Reserved.

No part of this publication may be reproduced, stored in a retrieval system, or transmitted, in any form or by any means without the prior written permission of the publisher, nor be otherwise circulated in any form of binding or cover other than that in which it is published and without similar condition being imposed on the subsequent purchaser.

If there are any errors or omissions in copyright acknowledgements the publisher will be pleased to insert the appropriate acknowledgement in any subsequent printing of this publication.

Although we have taken all reasonable care in researching this book we make no warranty about the accuracy or completeness of its content and disclaim all liability arising from its use

Table of Contents

Walt Disney World 6
    Culture 8
    Location & Orientation 9
    Climate & When to Visit 10

Sightseeing Highlights 12
    Magic Kingdom 12
    Epcot 14
    MGM Hollywood Studios 16
    Animal Kingdom 17
    Typhoon Lagoon 19
    Blizzard Beach 20
    Universal Studios 21
    Islands of Adventure 23
    The Wizarding World of Harry Potter 24
    SeaWorld 25
    La Nouba (Cirque du Soleil) 27
    Holy Land Experience 28
    John F. Kennedy Space Center (Cape Canaveral) 29

Recommendations for the Budget Traveler 30
    Places to Stay 30
        Animal Kingdom Lodge, Lake Buena Vista 31
        The Peabody Orlando 32
        Radisson Hotel Orlando 33
        Wyndham, Lake Buena Vista 33
        Hilton Orlando 34
    Places to Eat & Drink 35
        Les Chefs de France, France Pavilion, Epcot 35
        Victoria and Albert's, Orlando 36
        The Ravenous Pig, Winter Park 37
        Le Cellier, Canada Pavilion, Epcot 38
        Earl of Sandwich, Lake Buena Vista 38
    Places to Shop 39
        The Mall at Millenia, Orlando 39
        The Florida Mall, Orlando 40
        Orlando Premium Outlets 40

  Festival Bay Mall, Orlando 41
  Downtown Disney, Lake Buena Vista 42

Florida Keys 43
Culture 45
Location & Orientation 47
Climate & When to Visit 49

Sightseeing Highlights 51
Key Largo 51
  John Pennekamp Coral Reef State Park 51
  Everglades National Park 53
  Everglades Alligator Farm 54
  Florida Keys Wild Bird Center 55
  Dolphins Plus 56
  African Queen 56
Key West 58
  Ernest Hemingway Home & Museum 58
  Harry Truman's "Little White House" 59
  Key West Butterfly & Nature Conservatory 61
  Basilica of St. Mary Star of the Sea 62

Recommendations for the Budget Traveler 63
Places to Stay 63
  Marina del Mar 63
  The Pelican 64
  Hampton Inn Manatee Bay 65
  La Te Da 65
  The Truman Hotel 66
Places to Eat 67
  Key Largo Conch House 67
  Mrs. Mac's Kitchen 68
  Robert is Here 69
  Caribbean Club 70
  Mangia Mangia 71
  La Creperie 71
Places to Shop 72
  Key Largo Chocolates 72
  Shell World 73
  Mel Fisher's Key West Treasure Chest 74
  Bahama Village 75
  Duval Street 76

Walt Disney World

In the heart of central Florida you will find one of the most magical places on earth. Walt Disney World is beloved by adults and children as an exciting vacation destination. With four of the world's best theme parks and two water parks as well as dozens of other major attractions, Disney World in Orlando is the epicenter for vacation excitement, providing endless fun for everybody.

There are four main parks in Walt Disney World: Magic Kingdom, MGM Studios, Epcot, and the Animal Kingdom. In addition to these four main attractions there are two premium Disney water parks: Typhoon Lagoon and Blizzard Beach.

Magic Kingdom is the central focus of the Disney World Experience. This is the most recognized emblem of the Disney theme parks and it contains the majestic Cinderella's Castle and dozens of unique rides. MGM Studios is dedicated to Disney's incredible film history, with its own version of Hollywood Boulevard and tributes to the classic stars of decades past.

Epcot is an educational and fun trip around the world. It's a theme park dedicated to the diversity of world culture, and a visit there is the equivalent to an adventure in globalism. Animal Kingdom is an animal themed zoological extravaganza that showcases many diverse species and natural life from around the world.

The sheer magnitude of attractions in Orlando is overwhelming, and the energy of this vibrant city is incredible. You could spend a month here and never get to visit and enjoy everything this city has to offer. So if you're looking for a fulfilling entertainment experience that exceeds your (and your children's) wildest dreams, Walt Disney World is the ideal place for you.

Culture

Florida is a world-famous vacationland. Tourists travel from all over the world to come to this magical place to enjoy themselves. It is a travel destination that has a reputation for "anything goes" and Floridians are among the most laid back people on the planet. There are few rules, little pretension, and you're not expected to be anyone or do anything. Instead you can enjoy yourself, so kickback, relax, and see the sights alongside people who have lived there for their entire lives.

Orlando itself is no different. Everywhere you go you will see visitors and families experiencing the vacation of a lifetime. It exists as a microcosm of civilization dedicated to ensuring that everyone has an unforgettable experience. Furthermore, it contains one of the highest densities of theme parks and attractions in the world, but at the same time possesses some of the most remarkable food and shopping available in the United States. It may be hard to believe that a place can be so focused on enjoyment for the whole family; but it's true!

Because of its international appeal, Orlando is a place that contains a diversity of influences. There is no true "Orlandian," because most everyone who comes here has come from somewhere else. Because of this, it has developed a rich, international, multicultural vibe that adds to its allure. In Orlando, Florida, everybody is welcome. It doesn't matter what your history or background is.

Floridians are a friendly, ambitious people. They love to party, and revel in the moment. When you're in Orlando, you become swept away with seizing the day - the world that exists outside of this city for some reason isn't as important. Everyone is always looking for the next best thing, listening to new music, eating at exciting restaurants, searching for fun of all sorts. No matter if you're 5 or 50, Orlando is a epicenter of sensory stimulation that's mind-blowing, and absolutely wonderful.

Location & Orientation

Orlando is in the center of the southeastern state of Florida in the United States. It is 2 hours equidistant from both the Atlantic Ocean and Gulf of Mexico, 4 hours from the nearby state of Georgia, and 4 hours from the popular international city of Miami. Orlando features a major international airport. Alternative airports to fly into when visiting are Tampa and Miami International.

The population of Orlando is perpetually in flux. Because it is a premier vacation destination, the city tends to swell year-round, including both the (very hot) summer, and (hot) winter seasons. It is at least two hours from beaches, but Walt Disney World provides for this inconvenience by providing the public with two impressive water parks.

Walt Disney World itself is situated all over the city of Orlando, extending into the nearby district of Lake Buena Vista. Because of the incredible size of the parks, they established them outside the city so as not to interfere with urban lifestyle. Yet, they are easily accessible from interstate I-4. Many hotels offer shuttle services to the parks as well. Access to a car is preferable to relying on public transport.

Climate & When to Visit

The state of Florida has a sub-tropical climate with a wet season and a dry season. Orlando is also the lightning capital of the world. Temperatures range from 40 - 70 degrees Fahrenheit in winter, and 75-100 degrees Fahrenheit in summer. During the late summer months it is very humid, and tends to rain every afternoon.

July and August brings droves of visitors to Walt Disney World, and the lines seem to extend for miles. The worst time to be in Orlando is during mid to late summer, as everything is more expensive and overcrowded. Also, you may want to avoid visiting in mid-March, as this is Spring Break for schools all over the United States. During this period, students flock to Florida for some fun in the sun, causing the city to swell with hundreds of thousands of extra people.

So, if you're looking to beat the heat, the rain, and the crowds, visit Walt Disney World in September or October. Kids have gone back to school, people have returned to work, hurricane season is ending, and the lines (queues) will be shorter. This is the absolute best time to be there if you want a Walt Disney World experience that's worthwhile. Don't put yourself through the unnecessary hassle of thunderstorms and masses of summer tourists, go at a time where you can see everything at your convenience, and with better prices.

Sightseeing Highlights

Magic Kingdom

1180 7 Seas Dr,
Lake Buena Vista, FL 32830
(407) 824-4321
disneyworld.disney.go.com/parks/magic-kingdom/

Magic Kingdom is the most famous theme park of the Walt Disney World Orlando empire, and with 17 million visitors each year, it is the most visited theme park in the world.

It is the home of the iconic Cinderella's Castle, dozens of creative rides, and is truly one of the most magical places on earth for the children and their lucky parents.

Upon entry to the park you will enter into Disney's "Opening Credits" on Main Street. It's decorated in the style of early 20th century America and contains distinctive nuances from regions all over the country, with buildings named after the the park's contributors and figures from Disney's history. There are multiple sections in the park: Adventureland, Frontierland, Liberty Square, Fantasyland, and Tomorrowland.

Adventureland showcases foreign exploration, particularly after the stylings of the Swiss Family Robinson. It resembles dense forests and jungles that would be seen in the various regions of the world. Frontierland is the demonstration of the American Wild West. Old Cowboy movies come to life in this section; and also, Frontierland is host to a number of rides, including "Splash Mountain."

Liberty Square is representational of the American Colonial age, and hosts the Haunted Mansion ride. Fantasyland is the section aimed for those who are forever young, with the focus being a carnival. The iconic "It's a Small World" ride can be found here. The last section of Magic Kingdom is Tomorrowland, which is set up as the world of the future, as it had been foreseen in the 1950s.

Standard admission to the park is $89 for adults and $83 for children. However, if you are planning to visit more than one theme park while in Orlando, there are bulk options available. A two day Park Hopper Ticket will grant you access to all theme parks for two days, plus use of the Disney mass transport system. The two day ticket costs $239, a three day ticket is $293, and so forth. Magic Kingdom is open every day from 9:00 am to 6:00 pm.

Epcot

1200 Epcot Resort Blvd.,
Lake Buena Vista, FL 32830
(407) 824-4321
disneyworld.disney.go.com/parks/epcot/

Walt Disney World often gains confused reviews because of its tendency to be "for children." This is not entirely accurate as can be most seen at Walt Disney theme park Epcot which attracts thousands of adults as well as their children. The park is dedicated to the exploration of international culture, and the recognition of world achievement. The term "Epcot" is an acronym which means "Experimental Prototype Community of Tomorrow." The site that Epcot sits upon was supposed to become a city of 20,000 residents under the tutelage of Walt Disney himself, but that never worked out. But now, the world has Epcot, a magnificent park that kids will appreciate, and adults will love.

The park contains two sections: Future World and World Showcase. Epcot is a permanent World's Fair, an exhibition of many of the major countries of the world. Future World contains the emblematic symbol of Epcot, the geodesic sphere that holds the ride Spaceship Earth. The ride takes guests on a tour of the technological achievements of man from the prehistoric era to the 21st Century.

The World Showcase is a circle of pavilions laid out around a central lake in the park. The countries represented are Mexico, Norway, China, Germany, Italy, America, Japan, Morocco, France, the UK, and Canada. These stands contain themed shops and shows which highlight the distinctive and best features of each country, and are even staffed by members of the country represented.

Standard admission to the park is $89 for adults and $83 for children. However, if you are planning to visit more than one theme park while in Orlando, there are bulk options available. A two day <u>Park Hopper Ticket</u> will grant you access to all theme parks for two days, plus use of the Disney mass transport system. The two day ticket costs $239, a three day ticket is $293, and so forth. Future World is open every day from 9:00 and 9:00 pm, and the World Showcase opens at 11:00 am until 9:00 pm.

MGM Hollywood Studios

351 South Studio Dr.
Lake Buena Vista, FL 32830
(407) 824-4321
http://disneyworld.disney.go.com/parks/hollywood-studios/

Disney's MGM Studios (Hollywood Studios) is modeled after the romantic age of film, the 1930s and 40s, and is designed to appear like a movie set from that era. The theme park is also distinctive as Disney's Hollywood Studios boasts one of the best live music scenes in Disney World. However, like the rest of Walt Disney World, there are multiple themed sections within the territory of the park: Hollywood Boulevard, Echo Lake, Streets of America, Animation Courtyard, Pixar Place, and Sunset Boulevard.

Hollywood Boulevard is the first thing you come across after entering the park. Throughout the year visitors can watch parades along the road, and the avenue is modeled after Magic Kingdom's Main Street U.S.A. Hollywood Boulevard is lined with dozens of stores offering Disney merchandise. Echo Lake, is centered around an artificial lagoon. This section is the site of the "American Idol Experience" and "Star Tours."

Streets of America shows the streets of San Francisco and New York, and is home to a number of live stunt shows and movie set adventures. Animation Courtyard is, like its name suggestion, the section of the park dedicated to the development of famous animated Disney characters, and explores the legacy of Walt Disney himself.

Pixar Place is the most recent addition to Disney's Hollywood Studios, and is modeled after the Pixar Animation Studios of California with the focus on the film Toy Story. Lastly, Sunset Boulevard hosts the most exhilarating rides found on site: "Aerosmith's Rock 'N' Roller Coaster" and the "Tower of Terror."

Standard admission to the park is $89 for adults and $83 for children. However, if you are planning to visit more than one theme park while in Orlando, there are bulk options available. A two day Park Hopper Ticket will grant you access to all theme parks for two days, plus use of the Disney mass transport system. The two day ticket costs $239, a three day ticket is $293. Disney's Hollywood Studios is open daily from 9:00 am to 9:00 pm.

Animal Kingdom

1200 East Savannah Circle
Lake Buena Vista, FL 32830
(407) 939-6382
disneyworld.disney.go.com/parks/animal-kingdom

Animal Kingdom is a remarkable animal theme park located at Disney World, and the fourth park built at Walt Disney World.

Its subject is animal and ecological conservation, a theme espoused by Walt Disney himself. As a result of this exemplary vision, Animal Kingdom has gained accreditation from the Association of Zoos and Aquariums. The park contains seven specified areas, with the focal point being a 14-story artificial tree called the "Tree of Life," which is also the emblem of the park.

The themed sections of the park are Oasis, Discovery Island, Camp Minnie-Mickey, Africa, Rafiki's Planet Watch, Asia, and DinoLand U.S.A. Construction of a new section of the park modeled after the blockbuster film Avatar has also begun, and should be completed by 2014.

Oasis marks the entrance to the park, and one of the main sites for ongoing animal habitats at Animal Kingdom, including animals such as Scarlet Macaws and African Spoonbills. In the center of the park lies Discovery Island, which connects to almost every other section of the park, and contains the iconic Tree of Life. Camp Minnie-Mickey is a prime spot for kids, modeled after a summer camp. The highlight of this section is the energetic "Festival of the Lion King" show.

Africa and Rafiki's Planet Watch are connected, and feature some of the broadest diversity of animal life in the park. It is a practical Safari, where people can view hundreds of animals in their natural habitat. Asia is similar to Africa in the sense that it is set in a fictional village, and contains animals from that region. But, this section possesses Animal Kingdoms predominant roller coaster, Expedition Everest.

Standard admission to the park is $89 for adults and $83 for children. However, if you are planning to visit more than one theme park while in Orlando, there are bulk options available. A two day Park Hopper Ticket will grant you access to all theme parks for two days, plus use of the Disney mass transport system. The two day is $239, a three day is $293. Animal Kingdom is open daily from 9:00 am to 7:00 pm.

Typhoon Lagoon

1494 E Buena Vista Dr.,
Lake Buena Vista, FL 32830
(407) 939-6244
disneyworld.disney.go.com/parks/typhoon-lagoon/

Home to the world's largest indoor wave pool, Typhoon Lagoon is a Walt Disney World themed water park that is distinctive from many other aquatic vacation destinations around the world. It is modeled to resemble a tropical paradise that has been demolished after a typhoon, and shipwrecks, fishing gear, and other seafaring essentials are strewn about haphazardly. It is fascinating, energetically wet, and with more than 2 million visitors annually it is the most visited water theme park in the world.

There are multiple sections at Typhoon Lagoon, each with various attractions: Mount Mayday, Hideaway Bay, Typhoon Lagoon, Shark Reef, and Castaway Creek. The park is home to dozens of rides, varying in intensity in order to accommodate a diversity of visitors and ages, many white sandy beaches for lounging in the sun, a number of snack bars and cafes, and small beach shops. Amenities exist for guests such as rental lockers and restrooms.

Typhoon Lagoon is open daily from 9:00 am to 8:00 pm. Price of admission is $89 for Adults and $83 for children, but if you are planning to visit other Disney Parks in the area, there is a Magic Your Way option where package tickets can be bought for a premium discount.

Blizzard Beach

1534 Blizzard Beach Drive
Lake Buena Vista, FL 32830
(407) 560-3400
disneyworld.disney.go.com/parks/blizzard-beach

Blizzard Beach is the smaller of the two Walt Disney World themed water parks, but its uniqueness more than makes up for its size. The theme is from a Disney World fictional legend. According to the story, an unprecedented snow storm hit Orlando and lasted long enough for people to build Florida's first ski resort; but of course, the heat came and melted the snow, turning the former ski paradise into a snow beach. Throughout the park ski equipment can be seen stuck in the snow.

There are three main sections at Blizzard Beach (slopes): Green Slope, Purple Slope, and Red Slope. They can all be accessed from the top of Mount Gushmore, a 90 foot mountain and the centerpiece of the water park. Each section has a number of creative water rides, varying in difficulty. "Summit Plummet," found at Green Slope, is the most popular attraction. It stands at 120 feet and is the fastest freefall water slide in the world, dropping riders at speeds of up to 60 miles per hour.

Basic amenities such as restrooms, rental lockers, sun beds, and small eateries are also available to guests throughout the park. Blizzard Beach is open to the public daily from 9:00 am to 8:00 pm. Like the rest of the Disney parks, admission is $89 for adults and $83 for children. But discount tickets are available if purchased as a package (see above).

Universal Studios

6000 Universal Blvd,
Orlando, FL
(407) 363-8000
www.universalstudios.com/

The American Theme Park Universal Studios, Orlando, is a lively park based on the entertainment industry of Hollywood and elsewhere.

A visit to the park is like taking a trip back through the movies of yesteryear, and hosts many creative attractions to this affect. Within the park are six themed areas which surround a lagoon. The lagoon itself is famous for the Cinematic Spectacular, a live show displaying America's vibrant movie history. Universal Studios Orlando is one of the most original theme parks in Orlando, and a great day trip during your visit to the area.

Production Central marks the entrance to the theme park and contains a number of sound stages. Many of the park's live shows take place here. The second themed section is New York, and true to name actually resembles the city in form and architecture. Here guests can find rides such as "Twister" and "The Mummy."

San Francisco is the next section modeled after the Northern Californian city. San Francisco is home to "Jaws: the Ride" and the live show "Fear Factor Live!" The next section, World Expo, showcases world modernism and possesses two major park rides: "Men in Black: Aliens Attack!" and "The Simpsons Ride." The 6th theme is for the young ones, Woody Woodpecker's Kidzone; and the last, Hollywood, is dedicated to noteworthy landmarks from Hollywood's dynamic history. This section boasts iconic models of Schwab's Drug Store and Mel's Drive-In.

The park is open from 9:00 am daily, and closing times vary. The adjacent Universal City Walk is open from 11:00 am to 2:00 pm. Admission to the one park is $88. If you are planning to stay longer and visit more, however, it is much cheaper to buy multi-park and multi-day tickets all at once. It reduces the prices by up to 40% (see above).

Islands of Adventure

6000 Universal Blvd, Orlando, FL
(407) 363-8000
http://www.universalorlando.com/Theme-Parks/Islands-of-Adventure.aspx

Across the courtyard from the entrance to Universal Studios Orlando lies Universal's other Orlando attraction, Islands of Adventure. Where its neighbor is subdued, more family friendly, Islands of Adventure is a thrill ride ready to exhilarate your senses. With seven themed sections, several dazzling roller coasters, and dozens of premiere attractions, a trip to Islands of Adventure is a day spent in excitement.

You begin your quest at the Port of Entry, a standard port call sensation with a number of markets and restaurants. It is here that the emblematic symbol of Islands of Adventure is located: Pharos lighthouse. From there guests embark to Marvel Super Hero Island, where some of the most exhilarating rides are housed, most notably the "Incredible Hulk" and "Spiderman" roller coasters. The next place is Toon Lagoon, which is geared towards lighter themed content, and more kid friendly.

Islands of Adventure also contains Jurassic Park, with dinosaur-themed attractions; the Lost Continent, with a focus on the legends of ancient times (Greece, Arabia, Egypt, etc.); Seuss Landing, which is the park's haven for small children; and lastly, the Wizarding World of Harry Potter.

The park is open from 8:00 am daily to 9:00 pm. Admission to the one park is $88. If you are planning to stay longer and visit more, however, it is much cheaper to buy multi-park and multi-day tickets all at once. It reduces the prices by up to 40% (see above).

The Wizarding World of Harry Potter

6000 Universal Studios Plaza
Orlando, FL 32819
(954) 558-1784
www.harrypotterworldorlando.com

The most recent addition to Universal Studios Orlando's Islands of Adventure, the Wizarding World of Harry Potter, is reason alone to visit the exciting theme park. Winner of awards for the best new theme park and best new ride, "Harry Potter and the Forbidden Journey," The Wizarding World of Harry Potter offers you a chance to wander through the fantastical world of J.K. Rowling, and immerse yourself in the realm of wizardry.

The two main attractions of the brilliantly themed section are the lifelike replica of the fictional town of Hogsmeade, and the incredible rides. In Hogsmeade, you are able to taste Butter Beer and Pumpkin Juice at "The Three Broomsticks" restaurant the way that Harry Potter himself would have in Rowling's masterwork. Also in the model town, you can find Ollivanders, Zonko's Joke Shop, and the famous sweet shop Honeydukes.

Although the park is home to a number of unique rides such as the "Flight of the Hippogriff" and "Dragon Challenge", undoubtedly, the best ride at the park is "Harry Potter and the Forbidden Journey." The ride simulates a tour of Hogwarts castle, and participants have the opportunity to meet a number of characters along the way, including Dumbledore and the Whomping Willow.

A trip to the Wizarding World of Harry Potter is a day of excitement for children of all ages. Admission is included in your Islands of Adventure ticket, but look for discounts for multi-park passes and multi-day tickets (see above). In Orlando, it's always better to book in advance and buy multiple tickets at once.

SeaWorld

7007 Sea World Drive
Orlando, FL 32821
(888) 800-5447
seaworldparks.com/en/seaworld-orlando

Have you ever wanted to see Shamu? Ride with Dolphins? Get lost in one of Florida's best Marine zoos? Then Sea World Orlando is the place for you. Opened in 1973, Sea World Orlando offers a unique zoological aquatic experience complete with attractions, exotic animals, and a world of fun. The park is not separated into unique islands, per se, but there are themed sections. These include: Key West, Shamu's Happy Harbor, The Waterfront at SeaWorld, and the Wild Arctic.

Just as its name suggests, Key West is modeled after the same city in the Florida Keys. It possesses colorful tropical landscaping and a freshwater aquarium filled with Manta Rays. The next section, Shamu's Happy Harbor, is always the highlight of SeaWorld parks, especially for children. It is here that you can find the ubiquitous killer whale live show, where the park's mascot can show off tricks in front of a large audience.

The Waterfront at SeaWorld is a recent addition to the park, but it's also an excellent one. It is modeled after an idyllic Mediterranean village and contains an exciting ride called the "Sky Tower." Lastly, the Wild Arctic, is a showcase of marine life from the arctic north. It possesses an enormous indoor pavilion where guests can view Beluga whales and polar bears in a simulated habitat.

The park is open year round and hosts <u>live shows</u> that rotate according to season. The park hours are 9:00 am to 7:00 pm. It is recommended that you visit during feeding time, because this is when the animals are most active - the front desk will have this info each morning. Prices to enter are $74.99 for adults and $66.99 for children. If you're planning on visiting Aquatica or Busch Gardens while in the area, discount multi-park tickets are available as well.

La Nouba (Cirque du Soleil)

Downtown Disney, Walt Disney World Resort,
Orlando, FL 32830
407-939-7600
http://www.cirquedusoleil.com/en/shows/lanouba/tickets/florida.aspx

The most exciting and successful musical circus extravaganza on earth is none other than the Cirque de Soleil. Orlando is home to a permanent performance of La Nouba in Downtown Disney. The show features world famous acrobats, dancers, and other talents, possessing a showmanship unlike anything you've ever seen.

La Nouba is performed in its own customized theatre adjacent to the Walt Disney World resort complex in Lake Buena Vista. The show's name originates from the French phrase "faire la nouba," which means "to party."

This vibrant performance is a celebration of human creativity and a tribute to the liveliness of the human spirit. Colorful costumes, ornate makeup, and creative lighting are utilized to make an evening watching La Nouba an unforgettable experience. Permanent acts include the high wire, Chinese Diabolos, Aerial Ballet, and many more. It is a spectacular event both mind blowing and sensational, and a must see during your stay in Orlando.

Tickets to the shows vary based on season, seating, and time of performance. The range is from $57 to $140. Tickets can be purchased directly from their website or over the phone. And make sure to ask them for hot deals, because occasionally they do run specials.

Holy Land Experience

4655 Vineland Road, Orlando, FL 32811
(407) 872 2272
http://www.holylandexperience.com/

This unique theme park was formed by a Christian not for profit organization in 2001. The Holy Land Experience offers guests a trip into the world of the Bible, featuring exhibits of ancient Jerusalem as a living Biblical museum.

It is set up as a walled city, and upon entry you are greeted by the sights of a different world. The architecture within the walls is based off those of more than 2000 years ago, and exhibits include monuments of Christian historical significance: i.e. The Garden Tomb, The Dead Sea Caves of Qumran, and the Wilderness Tabernacle.

Visitors can see staff members moving around in period dress, ready to answer questions and tell stories when prompted. The Holy Land Experience is, astonishingly, also an active church site. Thus, the museum is affiliated with the Church of All Nations. But, even if you're not religious, the experience offers a unique perspective on the history of long ago, one that's educational and dramatic.

Admissions to the theme park are $40 for adults and $25 for children. The park is open Tuesday through Saturday from 10:00 am to 6:00 pm.

John F. Kennedy Space Center (Cape Canaveral)

SR 405, Kennedy Space Center, FL, 32899
(866) 737-5235
www.nasa.gov/kennedy/

Although not located in Orlando, the John F. Kennedy Space Center is an attraction you can't miss during your trip to the area. This magnificent United States Space Center at Cape Canaveral has been the launch site for every NASA space journey, without exception, since 1968.

It was John F. Kennedy's dream to get the United States' space program off the ground, and as a result of his ambition, the U.S. was the first to put a man on the moon in July 1969. That famous flight was launched from Cape Canaveral.

Visitors to the space center can tour the grounds, including NASA's launch and landing platforms, meet an astronaut, see rockets up close, walk through the U.S. Astronaut Hall of Fame, or if you're lucky, view a launch.

John F. Kennedy Space Center is open daily from 9:00 am to 6:00 pm. Admission prices are $50 for adults, and $40 for children. Ticket prices include the Hall of Fame, Bus tour, and IMAX space films.

Recommendations for the Budget Traveler

Places to Stay

Because of the plentiful attractions, visitors from all over the world come to Orlando year round to experience the entertainment on offer.

As a result, hotels in the city are plentiful, affordable, and possess unique characteristics that ensure your stay will be a great one. Competition in Orlando has forced the quality of accommodations to skyrocket, and the prices to drop, much to the benefit of the guests. With so many amazing options, it would be hard to go wrong.

Animal Kingdom Lodge, Lake Buena Vista

2901 Osceola Parkway, Lake Buena Vista, Orlando, FL 32830
(407) 938-3000
disneyworld.disney.go.com/resorts/animal-kingdom-lodge
$250-$400

Although a tad pricier than most hotels in the area, the character of this stunning Disney World Resort Hotel is unparalleled. Guests can recline in a luxurious rustic themed room, dine at the exemplary on site restaurant, or sit back and watch African wildlife through the windows of your room. That's right, Animal Kingdom Lodge is situated within the theme park, allowing visitors the unique immersion experience akin to being on African Safari. It's Disney's finest resort, without a doubt, and well worth the price.

The Peabody Orlando

9801 International Drive, Orlando, FL 32819
(407) 352-4000
www.peabodyorlando.com
$115-$150

One of the most reliable, well-reviewed hotels in Orlando, the Peabody offers comfortable accommodations at affordable prices. This hotel offers a sophisticated elegance, necessary amenities without pretension, and a friendly hotel staff who is more than willing to assist you in whatever you need.

The rooms are spacious, and its location on International Drive makes is adjacent to prime shopping and dining in Orlando.

Radisson Hotel Orlando

12799 Apopka Vineland Rd, Orlando, FL 32836
(407) 597-3400
www.radisson.com/lakebuenavistafl
$70-$120

This hotel is marvelous for one simple reason: it's on Walt Disney World's doorstep. Situated only a quarter mile from the parks, the Radisson Hotel Orlando is a fantastic place to stay while visiting Orlando. It is geocentric to everything of note, including Universal Orlando, SeaWorld, and shopping; and plus, it's a great hotel. At the Radisson, you can be close to everything you want to see, and relax in style and comfort. But, if you want to stay in this excellent place, make sure you book early. Rooms are inexpensive, and as a result, tend to fill up quickly.

Wyndham, Lake Buena Vista

1850 Hotel Plaza Blvd., Lake Buena Vista, Florida 32830
(407) 828-4444
http://www.wyndhamlakebuenavista.com/
$60-$120

The Wyndham at Lake Buena Vista is a great choice of accommodation for your Orlando vacation.

Located next door to Downtown Disney, a stay at Wyndham puts you in the center of the energetic nightlife and city excitement. The food is exemplary, the rooms are clean, and the views are magnificent. It is said that you can even see the fireworks at the Disney World theme parks from your windows. If you want to stay in comfort without sacrificing location, then Wyndham in Lake Buena Vista is the place for you.

Hilton Orlando

6001 Destination Parkway,
Orlando, FL 32819
407-313-4300
www.thehiltonorlando.com/
$90-$140

This fun hotel is noted for being family friendly, and for having one of the largest, most well-designed pool areas of all the hotels in Orlando. Kids and adults both love this great hotel, as it comes outfitted with restaurants (a steakhouse), cabanas, water slides, sports areas, and much more. The rooms are also clean and spacious, and the staff is friendly and helpful. All of your needs will be met, and you're sure to have a memorable time if you choose Hilton Orlando for your stay in the area.

Places to Eat & Drink

Food offerings in Orlando showcase flavorings from regions all over the world. Orlando is an international city, and thus, chefs come to central Florida to prepare amazing food for a global audience. Everything from classic American fare, to French, to even Moroccan is available in this vibrant city. The food culture it possesses is merely a culture of food - or, more specifically, excellent food.

Les Chefs de France, France Pavilion, Epcot

1200 Epcot Resort Blvd.,
Lake Buena Vista, FL 32830
(407) 939-3463
http://disneyworld.disney.go.com/dining/les-chefs-de-france/
$35-$60

This exquisite French restaurant in the Walt Disney Theme park in Lake Buena Vista offers a dining experience so delicious it will have you wanting more. Rich creamy soups, succulent meat, fresh baked breads, and decadent chocolate desserts are offered here beneath the France Pavilion at Les Chefs de France. One of the best things about visiting Epcot is eating the food, and some of the best food at Epcot is French, undoubtedly.

Victoria and Albert's, Orlando

Disney's Grand Floridian Resort and Spa, WDW 4401 Grand Floridian, Orlando, FL 32830-8416
(407) 939-3463
http://victoria-alberts.com/
$41-$120

Widely reviewed as one of the best restaurants in Florida, let alone in Orlando, Victoria and Alberts is a fine dining experience that's other-worldly.

The staff is professional, the chefs are eccentric, and the fare is creative and unforgettable. One of the popular offerings of this establishment is a nine course tasting meal, where the chef will pass before you a wealth of options you can't find anywhere else in the country.

The Ravenous Pig, Winter Park

1234 North Orange Avenue
Winter Park, FL 32789
(407) 628-2333
http://www.theravenouspig.com/
$15-$25

What's offered at this restaurant? Meat, meat, and meat. Vegetarians beware, the offerings at the Ravenous Pig will make you change your mind. The Ravenous Pig is undoubtedly one of the best restaurants in the area, and its meat-centric menu is dripping with savory flair. Whether you decide to eat a burger, or go all out for the steak and gruyere biscuits, your taste buds will praise you for your marvelous choice of restaurant.

Le Cellier, Canada Pavilion, Epcot

1200 Epcot Resort Blvd., Lake Buena Vista, FL 32830
(407) 939-3463
http://disneyworld.disney.go.com/dining/le-cellier-steakhouse/
$35-$60

Whoever thought a steakhouse with a Canadian theme would be a hit was an absolute genius. This original restaurant at the Canada Pavilion at Epcot offers up some of the most delectable menu options in the whole of Orlando, and gives visitors yet another reason to visit Walt Disney World. Undoubtedly, the best thing on the menu here is the Wild Mushroom Filet Mignon. If you pair it with the Canadian Cheddar Cheese Soup you'll be in for the experience of a lifetime.

Earl of Sandwich, Lake Buena Vista

 1750 East Buena Vista Drive
Lake Buena Vista, FL 32830
(407) 938-1762
http://www.earlofsandwichusa.com/
$10-$15

This deli makes the list of recommended restaurants for the simple fact that it stands head and shoulders over all the competition.

Earl of Sandwich, located just outside of Disney World in Lake Buena Vista, serves up local, fresh ingredients to its customers. The sandwiches are placed on fresh baked bread, and meat and cheese and numerous toppings are piled high. And the prices are incredible for the amount of food you're given. For lunch, check out Earl of Sandwich. You'll be extremely happy you did.

Places to Shop

Orlando, Florida and the areas surrounding Walt Disney World is a paradise for shopping enthusiasts the world over. With great numbers of international malls, premium outlet centers, and bustling plazas you could shop 'til you drop and never see everything. For all the attractions existent in Orlando, many people visit this grand city just for the shopping alone. With everything from cutting edge designer labels, to independent clothing stores, to odds and ends and fascinating souvenir shops - there's something for everyone in Orlando, Florida.

The Mall at Millenia, Orlando

4200 Conroy Road
Orlando, FL
(407) 363-3555
http://www.mallatmillenia.com/

This designer mall in central Florida brings people in for hundreds of miles around to wander through its halls.

With over 150 stores, Millenia is an upscale premium indoor shopping mall, complete with restaurants, department stores, independent boutiques, and designer labels.

The Florida Mall, Orlando

8001 S Orange Blossom Trail
Orlando, Florida
(407) 851-7234
http://www.simon.com/

Orlando's Florida Mall is essentially Millenia Mall's other half. This indoor shopping mall contains almost 250 stores, and has a reputation of being less crowded than Millenia. The offerings here are less designer label, and more independent. It's also home to the famous M&M store.

Orlando Premium Outlets

8001 S Orange Blossom Trail
Orlando
(407) 851-7234
http://www.premiumoutlets.com/outlets/outlet.asp?id=96

One of the largest outlet malls in Florida, Orlando Premium Outlets houses hundreds of stores.

Its impressive outlay includes everything from Juicy Couture to Guess, and items from electronics to luggage to designer fashions. And, for your convenience, they have an amazing food court.

Festival Bay Mall, Orlando

5250 International Drive
Orlando, FL 32819
(407) 351-7718
http://www.shopfestivalbaymall.com/

Rounding out the triumvirate of the great Orlando malls, Festival Bay Mall offers all the amenities of the Milennia and Florida Malls, without the large crowds.

And because it is located on International Drive, it's close to many of the best restaurants in the city as well.

Downtown Disney, Lake Buena Vista

Post Office Box 10,000
Lake Buena Vista, FL 32830
(407) 939-2698
http://disneyparks.disney.go.com/downtown-disney/

This outrageous, alluring boardwalk near the Walt Disney Theme parks is the height of nightlife in Orlando. Hosting dozens of shops, restaurants, and clubs, an evening here is the epitome of what Orlando is all about. Stores here contain Disney paraphernalia, designer wear, novelty items, jewelry and tons more. And there's free parking, which is an added bonus.

Florida Keys

The Florida Keys is "America's Caribbean" and this peaceful part of the southeastern United States has a laid-back, island feel. Key West (in the south) and Key Largo (in the north) are the main towns. The area has been a popular vacation spot for the rich and famous for years, including presidents Harry S. Truman and Richard Nixon and literary figures, Ernest Hemingway and Tennessee Williams.

President Nixon had a second home in Key Biscayne, near Key Largo, from 1969 until the end of his Presidency in 1974. The home was torn down in 2004 and a new home built that bears no resemblance to the Nixon home.

In his day, Nixon used his Southern Florida White House at least fifty times, visiting his controversial friend "Bebe" Rebozo who lived nearby, and to escape the press during the height of the Watergate crisis. The home gained recognition again in 1983 when the Al Pacino movie "Scarface" was filmed there.

President Truman's "Little White House" is still standing and is open for tours, In addition to Truman, Presidents Roosevelt, Eisenhower, Kennedy and Carter all spent time in the Little White House at one time.

Playwright Tennessee Williams was a resident of the Florida Keys and finished a draft of "A Streetcar Named Desire" while staying at his home in Key West, which was his primary residence until his death in 1983. It is a private home and not open to the public. Ernest Hemingway's home, however, is open for tours and descendants of his six-toed cats still roam the property.

There is a rich movie history in the area as well, with classics like "Key Largo" and "The African Queen" being based here.

Key West and Key Largo offer many sea and nature-related activities, including swimming with dolphins or sea lions, spotting alligators or walking the nature trails.

It is a good idea to divide one's time between Key Largo and Key West, perhaps spending half your vacation in each location.

Two "musts" to eat in the area are key lime pie and conch. The pie is made from local limes which are smaller and more tart than regular limes. The pie is made in different ways by different restaurants but is always creamy and delicious, typically sitting atop a crunchy graham cracker crust.

Conch (pronounced "konk") is a sea animal popular in South Florida. Remember the large pink and white shells people hold to their ears to hear the sounds of the sea? These are empty conch shells. This sea mollusk has a distinctive and delicious taste and is served in salads, chowder, battered, or made into fritters.

With so much to see, do and eat, visitors will wonder why they waited so long to visit the Keys!

Culture

The Keys were originally populated by Native American Indians. Later, famed Spanish explorer Ponce de Leon officially "discovered" the area, thus the areas were given Spanish names. Key comes from the Spanish word "Cayo" or "island." Key West was originally called "Cayo Huesco", meaning Bone Island because it was believed to be an Indian burial ground. Key Largo's name came from "Cayo Largo" or "large island."

Key West was, and still is, the most populated of the Keys and the most prosperous. For many years, its wealth came in large part from treasures found in many nearby shipwrecks. Though Indians first lived in the area, in later years many Cuban exiles landed in Key West because of its proximity to their country. Immigrants from the nearby Bahamas also settled in the area. Because of this, in 1982 the U.S. Border Patrol set up roadblocks along Highway 1, to search for illegal immigrants and drugs being brought into Florida.

This practice seemed like a good idea but it caused a stir within the Key West City Council because members feared it would decrease the appeal of tourism. Then-Mayor Dennis Wardlow and the council declared their independence from the rest of Florida, calling the area the Conch Republic. Wardlow appointed himself Prime Minister and asked for $1 billion in "foreign aid". He didn't get the billion, but his actions attracted massive publicity and the roadblocks were removed. Today, drug trafficking is sadly still a problem, but some of the Key West residents still refer to this area as the Conch Republic.

Key West and Key Largo are rich in history, whether literary, presidential or seaworthy. The cultures of America, Cuba, the Bahamas and all of the Caribbean blend together to make a trip to the Keys an exotic experience of music, food and fun.

Location & Orientation

The Florida Keys are actually a series of small islands in the Southeastern tip of Florida that were created during the Ice Age, when melting glaciers exposed coral reefs and land. The two largest Keys are Key Largo, a 33-mile-long stretch of land, in the Upper Keys closer to Miami, and the 4-mile-long Key West, the farthest south of Miami and only 90 miles from Cuba. In fact, Key West boasts of being the U.S. city that's the farthest south of anywhere, though the claim is often debated.

About 130 miles of U.S. Highway 1, also called the Overseas Highway, connects all of the Keys and is a very popular means of navigating the area. An important tip for drivers or those seeking directions to an address is the Mile Marker (MM) system, used up and down the Overseas Highway. It may be the only address given for some locations, and if not, it will be added on to the main address in many cases.

The small green signs begin at MM 107 in Key Largo and get smaller in number until reaching Key West, which is MM 0. When asking directions to a location, residents may say, "It's at MM 68.5". There's no MM 68.5; there are only whole numbers, but they mean the spot lies in-between marker 68 and marker 69.

This southern area of Florida has become a popular port over the years, and many people arrive in the Keys by cruise ship, for a short, one-day adventure. Non-cruise passengers planning a more extended stay usually arrive by plane.

There is an airport in the Keys – Key West International (305-296-5439) - and it handles flights from other cities in Florida as well as Atlanta and a few other major cities nearby. However, it's not equipped for large jets from farther destinations, so most air passengers fly into Miami International Airport and either rent a car or take a shuttle or bus. Rental cars are available at the airport, except for Enterprise or Alamo, whose rental offices are located off site. The drive from the Miami airport to Key Largo, the closest large Key city, takes about 1½ hours in traffic.

Visitors not renting a car have several options for arriving in Key Largo. Airporter (305-852-3413) runs a shuttle for approximately $50 per person and Super Shuttle (305-871-2000 or www.supershuttle.com) makes the trip, too, for slightly more. Greyhound has the Keys Shuttle (800-231-2222 or 888-765-9997) also. Once in Key Largo, even visitors without a car will find plenty of taxis or buses to get around. A seven-day unlimited bus pass runs $8. Many visitors rent scooters or bikes in town.

Key West has an even better way to navigate around town. Old Town Trolley Tours (305-296-6688 or www.trolleytours.com) is a hop on-hop off service that serves two purposes. Stay on board and it's a great way to get an overview of the city, or visitors can get off at any of the 12 stops and then re-board later (every 30 minutes from 9 a.m. to 4:30 p.m.).

Tours originate at Mallory Square and Whitehead Street and the cost is $30 for adults and $27 for seniors or military members; children under 12 are free. If visitors retain their ticket, they may travel in the same way on a second consecutive day free of charge. Conch Tour Trains (888-916-8687) runs a similar service, beginning at Mallory Square and Front Street, and although they don't offer the second day free policy, they do give visitors a map and discount coupons towards area attractions.

No matter what method visitors use to arrive or navigate once reaching their destination, the best advice is to relax, enjoy the tropical atmosphere, soak up the seemingly endless rays of sunshine, and absorb the history, culture and fun that await them.

Climate & When to Visit

There are really only two seasons in the Florida Keys – wet and dry. A tropical climate is typical year-round and the area will feel more like the Caribbean than the rest of Florida does. The period from November to May is more dry and cool and June through October is when more heat and humidity will be felt, but much like the tropics, it is never entirely out of the question to feel heat and humidity.

Temperatures in the "cool" period average 66° F (19°C) to 81°F (27°C) and temperatures in the hot season average 76°F (24°C) to 90°F (32°C). Key Largo is more susceptible to the humidity than Key West and therefore the comfort level fluctuates more. The heat and humidity doesn't change much in Key West year-round. One worry for people throughout Florida, especially along the coast, is the tropical storm, tropical cyclone or hurricane. Hurricane season is at its peak from June to November and there are often warnings issued if a storm looks to be close to making landfall. Hurricane Georges in 1998, and Hurricane Katrina and Hurricane Wilma in 2005 all did considerable damage to the Keys.

In spite of weather incidents, there are festivals all year long that encourage locals to enjoy the event and entice tourists to visit. A major sailing event is held in January, February offers art shows and craft shows, food festivals are held in April and a lobster fest is celebrated in August. All the attractions are open no matter the time of year and would only be closed in the event of an imminent major storm, so visiting is never out of season.

Here is a link to the current and extended weather forecast for the Florida Keys:
http://www.weather.com/united-states/florida/florida-keys-23511750/

Sightseeing Highlights

Key Largo

John Pennekamp Coral Reef State Park

102601 Overseas Highway, MM 102.5, Key Largo, Florida 33037
305-451-6300
www.pennekamppark.com

This park is listed on the U.S. National Register of Historic Places and is the first park in the United States that is located undersea.

It is the only living reef made of coral to be found in the continental United States.

The location was named for late newspaper editor John D. Pennekamp, from Miami, who not only was instrumental in establishing the Everglades National Park, but also worked tirelessly to protect and keep the integrity of the coral reefs. Although the reefs are located underwater, there is much to see from above, as well, so there are activities for visitors interested in all levels of adventure. Even the visitor center is part of the attraction, with a 30,000 gallon aquarium on site featuring local and unusual fish.

The visitor center is open from 8 a.m. to 5 p.m. and these same hours apply to the activities, too.

For the most adventurous, there is scuba diving and snorkeling. Those who are already familiar with these activities will probably get the most out of the experience, but there are lessons available, too. Snorkelers and scuba divers will be able to actually travel underwater through the coral areas. Scuba diving lessons begin at 8:30 a.m., are $185 and take about 5 hours, and then immediately following, visitors can do an actual dive without their instructor. Already-experienced divers are able to dive at 9 a.m. or 1:30 p.m. for a fee of $55, naturally forgoing the lesson. For snorkeling, there are no lessons, so it is assumed that visitors are already capable, though it's possible to "rent" a guide for additional help. The snorkeling is $30 for adults and $25 for those under age 18, and lasts about 1½ hours. Equipment can be rented on the property.

Those who prefer to stay above water still have many activities, however. Walking trails will take visitors through the tropical vegetation of a natural mangrove area, with the chance to see many native birds. Kayaks ($17 an hour) or canoes ($20 an hour) can also be rented, for leisurely exploring the waters of the mangrove.

Another popular activity is the 2 ½-hour glass bottom boat ride that offers the opportunity to see the coral reefs from the comfort of a large boat. The cost is $24 for adults and $17 for children ages 4-11. Two beaches within the park offer the chance for simple sunbathing or relaxing, too.

Everglades National Park

Ernest Coe Visitors Center
40001 State Road 9336
Homestead, Florida 33034 (Key Largo)
305-242-7700
www.nps.gov/ever/index.htm

This is on the "must see" list for most visitors to the Keys and it's a UNESCO World Heritage Site. The park is home to many endangered species and has been classified as a wilderness area (the largest subtropical site in the United States).

This is the exotic and adventurous Florida Keys destination that most people think of, complete with marshland and alligators, as well as manatees, and birds including eagles and vultures. Bring insect repellent as mosquitoes and other bugs are serious business here, and dress for comfort, especially in the summer when temperatures are hot and humid.

Also bear in mind hurricane season from June to November, and the fact that this may affect whether the park is open or not. The park is normally open from 9 a.m. to 5 p.m. daily and there are walking trails for self-exploration or tours led by park rangers (recommended). The ranger tours are at 10:30 a.m. daily and they provide a one-hour wildlife walk and exploration – expect to see alligators! The visitor center has many displays about the park and its animals. There is a $10 fee per car to enter the park – no charge for tours.

Everglades Alligator Farm

40351 SW 192 Avenue
Homestead, Florida 33034
305-247-2628
www.everglades.com

For the more daring visitors who didn't get enough alligator time at Everglades National Park, there is another attraction nearby that is all about the 'gators. There are more than 2000 of them here, as well as snakes of many kinds. This attraction has a more organized feel to it, with alligator shows, alligator feeding times, and a snake show.

There are also airboat rides, and this is something people may have seen on various television shows over the years. The airboats glide over the waters and allow up close and personal glimpse of the alligators as visitors buzz along in safety. Airboat rides are available every 25 minutes after the hour, and the farm is open from 9 a.m. to 6 p.m. Tickets for the boat ride and the shows are $23 for adults and $16 for children; the shows only are $15 for adults and $11 for children.

Florida Keys Wild Bird Center

93600 Overseas Highway MM 93.6
Tavernier, Florida 33070 – Key Largo
305-852-4486
www.kkwbc.org

This is not an amusement park but visitors who want to get close to birds of all kinds couldn't ask for a better attraction. This location rescues birds, rehabilitates those who are injured, and then prepares them for release into their own habitat again. It was founded by a Florida woman named Laura Quinn who spent 35 years rescuing local birds, until her death in 2010. Her work continues. A self-guided tour allows visitors to walk the paths and see owls, hawks, falcons, raptors, pelicans and vultures, among other birds, as they recuperate and grow stronger. Donations are accepted. The center is open from sunrise to sunset daily.

Dolphins Plus

31 Corrine Place
Key Largo, Florida 33037
866-860-7946
www.dolphinsplus.com

For many tourists, a trip to the Keys wouldn't be complete without an opportunity to swim with dolphins. This location offers that experience plus the opportunity to swim with a sea lion.

The dolphin experience includes time to get an introduction to dolphins in general, and then getting into the water with them and swimming or asking for particular commands to be done. The experience is about 2 hours long and the cost is $195. The sea lion experience is much the same and the cost is $150. Consult the web site for particulars regarding age or health of the visitor wishing to do the swim.

African Queen

Port Largo, U.S. Highway 1, Mile Marker 100 – Holiday Inn Docks, Key Largo, Florida 33037
305-451-8080
www.africanqueenflkeys.com

What a treat for classic film lovers who remember the 1951 movie "African Queen" with Humphrey Bogart and Katharine Hepburn!

This is the actual boat that was used during the filming, and visitors can take a canal cruise on it, with or without dinner. The British Railways Company built the boat in England in 1912 and prior to the making of the film, it was used to carry cargo, missionaries and hunting parties. But since its "African Queen" fame, it's been named a National Historic Site and now is reserved strictly for passengers.

The canal cruise takes 1½ hours and brings passengers from the marina through Port Largo's canals to the Atlantic Ocean and back again. The cost is $49 per person and cruises are at 10 a.m., noon, 2, 4 or 6 p.m. The dinner cruise is two hours long. Passengers board at the marina and begin the trip through Port Largo's canals, but they stop at the Pilot House restaurant, disembark and enjoy a three-course meal, then cruise back again. The cost is $89 and includes gratuities for the meal. Check with the web site for dinner times as they are flexible. In 1998, "African Queen" was ranked the 17th greatest film of all time by the American Film Institute, and Humphrey Bogart won the Best Actor Oscar in the 1950s for the film, so visitors may very much enjoy being a part of Hollywood history.

Key West

Ernest Hemingway Home & Museum

907 Whitehead Street
Old Town Key West, Florida 33040
305-294-1136
www.hemingwayhome.com

 The author of such classics as "For Whom the Bell Tolls", "A Farewell to Arms", "The Sun Also Rises" and "The Old Man and the Sea" lived and wrote here for more than 10 years, finding both the inspiration and the solace that he needed. Those years were the most productive of his career. A fellow writer told Hemingway about the Key West area when they were both in Paris.

In 1928, the author and his then wife Pauline moved to the area, at first living in an apartment above a Ford dealership (which is where he finished writing "A Farewell to Arms") and then finally moving into this home, which has been placed on the National Historic Landmark list. The Hemingways installed a pool – the first to be put into the ground in the Key West area in the 1930s. It was a costly venture and visitors to the home should look for a penny pressed into the cement surrounding the pool. At one point, Hemingway said to the contractor, "Here – take the last penny I've got!" and threw it at him, where it landed in the cement. The furnishings are original to the home and visitors will see one other unique feature.

It's well known that Hemingway loved cats. Among the cats he owned was one given to him by a ship's captain. The cat was named Snowball and had an extra toe on one foot. Needless to say, Snowball has long since passed away but descendants of that cat remain – in fact 40 of them – and many of them are also 6-toed. They wander the property at leisure. The home is open from 9 a.m. to 5 p.m. daily and there is a 30-minute guided tour. The gift shop and book store contain many souvenirs pertaining to the author, including copies of all of his novels. The admission is $13 for adults, $6 for children. Children age 5 and under are admitted free.

Harry Truman's "Little White House"

111 Front Street
Key West, Florida 33040
305-294-9911
www.trumanlittlewhitehouse.com

This home has had a varied and historical background. In 1890 it was a command headquarters for the Navy during the Spanish-American War, and it served in that capacity toward the beginning of World War II. It also was a location for government meetings through the years. When the 33rd President of the United States, Harry S. Truman, discovered it, he adopted it as his winter White House, beginning in 1946. From then until 1952 he spent as much time as possible there, hosting government functions and meetings.

Truman and other Cold War-era presidents after him used the location as a winter White House. In fact, today it is still occasionally used by government officials, and if so, the home is not available for touring.

But otherwise, tour guides happily take visitors through the home, giving them a look at the more personal side of Truman and in fact other presidents since him. There have been some renovations done on the property, but at least 90% of the furnishings and overall look of the home remain from the Truman time period. Tours are given seven days a week, departing every 20 minutes, from 9 a.m. to 4:30 p.m.

There is also a one-acre botanical garden on the property, with tropical plants and trees dating back to 1890. Touring the garden is on a self-guided basis and included in the admission price, which is $16 for adults, $14 for seniors, and $5 for children ages 5-12. Children under 5 are admitted free of charge.

Key West Butterfly & Nature Conservatory

1316 Duval Street
Key West, Florida 33040
305-296-2988 or 800-839-4647
www.keywestbutterfly.com

Entering this location is like finding true paradise, with tropical plants and trees and hundreds of butterflies and birds roaming freely as visitors walk among them in a glass-enclosed, climate-controlled environment. Nearly 60 species of butterflies from around the world flutter around, as well as 20 types of exotic birds.

The Learning Center at the entrance presents a 15-minute film regarding the butterfly and its life cycle, and live caterpillars are on display. The Conservatory is open from 9 a.m. to 5 p.m. daily. Admission is $12 for adults, $9 for children ages 4-12 and also for seniors and the military. Children under 4 are admitted free.

Basilica of St. Mary Star of the Sea

1010 Windsor Lane
Key West, Florida 33040
305-284-1018
www.keywestcatholicparish.org

Regardless of their religious beliefs, visitors have been flocking to this basilica and its surrounding grounds since 1851 to appreciate its history and its beauty. It is listed as a National Historic Site and is a popular pilgrimage site as well. The basilica is built on limestone rock and constructed of a combination of concrete, limestone, beach sand and coral.

Hurricanes and tropical storms have swirled all around the basilica and its grounds, toppling buildings through the years. Mysteriously (or perhaps not), Sr. Mary's has remained untouched. The first Mass of the day is celebrated at 7:30 a.m. and the basilica opens at that time. The grounds are open at any time and feature peaceful areas for relaxation.

One area is the Our Lady of Lourdes Stone Grotto, constructed in 1922 from natural rock from the area. Residents often gather here when hurricane warnings are issued, asking for protection. There are stone benches to sit and reflect. The Stations of the Cross Garden features lovely tropical plants and a rock garden, and there is a unique rosary stone path, resembling the shape of rosary beads. Regardless of one's religion, the formation and beauty of this path is worth a look. The convent next door now houses a group of nuns but it was a hospital during the Spanish-American War.

Recommendations for the Budget Traveler

Places to Stay

Marina del Mar

527 Caribbean Drive, Key Largo, Florida 33037
305-451-4107
www.marinadelmaarkeylargo.com

This property is located near to the Coral Reef Park. Its rooms include air conditioning, small refrigerators, a hair dryer, iron and ironing board, free internet, and coffee/tea makers.

There is a pool, gift shop and lobby safe deposit box. Rooms start at $161 and many discounts or specials are offered so it is best to consult the web site in advance.

The Pelican

99340 Overseas Highway
Key Largo, Florida 33037
305-451-3576
www.hungrypelican.com

This may not be the most elaborate hotel in Key Largo, but its rates are excellent, rooms are clean and comfortable, and there are a couple of interesting "extras", including complimentary continental breakfast from 7:30 to 9:30 a.m. daily. Another extra is the nearby Manatee Bay, and the availability of kayaks or canoes – free of charge – to guests who want to spend some time relaxing on the water. Rooms with two beds start at $110 and cottages with a kitchen start at $125.

Hampton Inn Manatee Bay

102400 Overseas Highway
Key Largo, Florida 33037
305-451-1400
www.hamptoninnkeylargo.com

This property boasts a location that's close to the Coral Reef Park, the African Queen and Everglades National Park. There is a gym, fitness center and pool on the property and the rooms offer internet service, a refrigerator, wet bar and HDTV.

Free hot breakfast is served daily. The hotel has several specials and discounts, so consult the web site prior to booking. King-sized rooms start at $227.

La Te Da

1125 Duval Street, Key West, Florida 33040
305-286-6706 Ext. 10 or 877-528-3320
www.lateda.com

Although this hotel is located on popular Duval Street, with its shops and restaurants, the property itself retains a relaxed island atmosphere. It is a small bed and breakfast (11 rooms total) and caters to adults to maintain a quiet sense of relaxation.

Rooms have a refrigerator, air conditioning, TV, internet, and there is a free daily breakfast. Rates start at $135 for a standard room with a king-sized bed or two queens. There is also a restaurant, bar and cabaret on the property, which resembles a large Florida mansion.

The Truman Hotel

611 Truman
Key West, Florida 33040
305-296-6700 or 866-4TRUMAN
www.trumanhotel.com

As a tribute to the fact that President Truman spent many years in Key West, this colorful and relatively new hotel in Old Town Key West bears his name.

It has an ideal location, one block from Duval Street and within walking distance to many attractions. Sundecks off the rooms offer wonderful views, and rooms feature wireless internet, free continental breakfast, nightly turndown service, and there is a pool on the property. Winter rates begin at $199 and Summer/Fall rates begin at $169 but the hotel offers discounts and specials.

Places to Eat

Key Largo Conch House

100211 Overseas Highway Mile Marker 100.2
Key Largo, Florida 33037
305-453-4844
www.keylargoconchhouse.com

This family-owned restaurant prides itself on good food, a friendly atmosphere, reasonable prices and homemade specials. They are open Monday through Friday from 11 a.m. to 9 p.m. and Saturday and Sunday from 8 a.m. to 10 p.m. Seafood is the specialty here, whether in a meal or a light lunch or snack. Lunch features include Panini's, wraps, soups and salads, all in the $7-15 range. Dinner choices include a fried seafood basket with a choice of the fresh catch of the day, shrimp, conch or mahi-mahi, with chips, for $12-14; salads average $9-16 including seafood salads; a complete meal of the fresh catch of the day, breaded conch or salmon averages $19-23. Save room for the homemade key lime pie. And wash it all down with one of their specialty craft beers.

Mrs. Mac's Kitchen

99336 Overseas Highway Mile Marker 99.4
Key Largo, Florida 33037
305-451-3722
www.mrsmacskitchen.com

This has been favorite among locals and tourists since 1968 and the restaurant has won many people's choice awards for its food and down-home atmosphere. Prices are reasonable and there is a huge menu selection. Lunch features include chili or conch chowder from $3-5, salads in the $8 range – either seafood or vegetable; "flying saucers", which are pita sandwiches, are $8; there are many burger choices and "baskets" of breaded crab, fish, shrimp or clams for $11.

Dinners are served from 5-9:30 p.m. and feature many of the same choices as at lunch, but in addition there are crab cakes, fish of the day, steak, chicken, ribs – all ranging from $10-19, plus nightly specials are plentiful. They offer homemade key lime pie slices for $4 and a key lime freeze for $3. The restaurant is open Monday through Saturday from 7 a.m. to 9:30 p.m.

Robert is Here

19200 SW 344th Street, Homestead, Florida 33034
305-246-1592
www.robertishere.com

This is a "don't miss" when driving around the various Key Largo sites. It's popular with tourists and locals alike and its story is charming.

Many years ago, a father started a stand selling fruits and vegetables. He sent his little son, Robert, to the side of the road to help sell the produce, but no one noticed the little guy. So the father painted a sign so people would see him and hopefully stop and make a purchase.

The sign said, "Robert is Here." Today, young Robert has become a grown man and he's taken over the business, still selling fruit and vegetables but also homemade jams and jellies. He's turned the stand into a large venue with live music on the weekends, a picnic area and a splash park for children. Refreshments made from his own produce include cold coconuts and milkshakes made from any fruit he sells – the most popular and delicious, according to customers, is the key lime milkshake. The property is open from 8 a.m. to 7 p.m., including holidays, but only from November to August.

Caribbean Club

Mile Marker 104 Bayside US Highway 1
Key Largo, Florida 33037
305-451-4466
www.caribbeanclubkl.com

Movie lovers will enjoy a stop here, since exterior shots for the classic "Key Largo" with Humphrey Bogart and Lauren Bacall were filmed here. Memorabilia from the movie are displayed inside.

This is more of a bar – frequented by many locals and tourists, too. The main feature is the drinks – reasonably priced. But they offer pub food (light snacks) and have spaghetti specials on certain nights (consult web site for updates). They also have special activities throughout the week: movie night, with screenings on the dock and hot dogs and popcorn available, karaoke night, and trivia night. A word of caution: Cash Only! No credit cards accepted. What started as a fishing retreat in 1938 has become world-famous thanks to the 1947 Warner Brothers movie. Open daily from 7 a.m. to 4 a.m.

Mangia Mangia

900 Southard Street
Key West, Florida 33040
305-294-2469
www.mangia-mangia.com

This is an Italian restaurant that incorporates Florida seafood into many of its dishes. They offer many salads and soups in the $6-9 range, plus many forms of pasta and sauce, from $13-20, including sauce with seafood, scallops, conch or mahi-mahi. Grilled salmon or chicken are other favorites, for $16-19, as is coconut shrimp or chicken in the same price range. Visit the web site and print out a 10% off coupon for your meal. They are open from 5:30 p.m. and the last seating is at 10:00 p.m.

La Creperie

300 Petronia Street, Key West, Florida 33040
305-517-6799
www.lacreperiekeywest.com

This Bahama Village-area restaurant is owned by two women from France who have put their cooking skills to great use in Florida, for a feeling that combines French cooking with the Florida/island feel. The restaurant resembles a French country mansion.

Many sandwiches are offered, as well as French coffee, homemade ice cream, and breakfasts such as Croque Monsieur (baked ham and cheese sandwich on croissant with salad). But the crepes will have visitors wanting to go back for more. There are perhaps 20 selections for fillings, including banana and lime, banana and coconut, raspberry and cream cheese, pineapple/coconut, or nutella.

A fun aspect is that there is counter seating where you can watch the crepes being made right in front of you. Most items range from $8-$11. The restaurant is open from 7:30 a.m. to 5 p.m. daily and can be crowded, but worth a slight wait.

Places to Shop

Key Largo Chocolates

100470 Overseas Highway, Key Largo, Florida 33047
305-453-6613
www.keylargochocolates.com

Owners Kristie and Bob Thomas began making their specialty chocolates in their own kitchen, but the business has expanded beyond their wildest dreams.

They don't just make chocolates, they combine the sweet with local ingredients, primarily fruits. Locals and tourists delight in their handmade truffles in flavors like banana daiquiri, Caribbean spice, coconut dark, Florida orange, key lime dark, mango and strawberry.

They also sell key lime pie on a stick – chocolate covered, of course! Another specialty is the "chocodile", in white, dark or milk chocolate – and an eerie replica of the many crocodiles found in the area. The store is located near Everglades National Park and is open from 10:30 a.m. to 8 p.m. daily.

Shell World

97600 Overseas Highway Mile Marker 97.5
Key Largo, Florida 33037
305-852-8245
www.shellworldflkeys.com

Yes, it's a bit touristy. But it's also pretty amazing in terms of the number of items available in the two-floor building. The selection is staggering and includes clothing, jewelry, cds of local musicians' music, greeting cards, and of course, shells – by themselves or used in the making of night lights, lamps, and any number of other items. Souvenir-seekers should be thrilled.

Mel Fisher's Key West Treasure Chest

200 Green Street
Key West, Florida 33040
305-296-9936 or 800-434-1399
www.melfisher.com and www.keywestchamber.org

Mel Fisher spent a lifetime seeking treasure from dives – bringing up to the surface items from shipwrecks that other people only dream about. Though Mel passed away, his legacy continues and his store features shipwreck coins, unusual and antique jewelry, other antique items and artifacts from lost ships. The store's schedule fluctuates and it's best to call in advance to make sure they are open. For an unusual gift or souvenir, this is the place.

Bahama Village

Bordered by Whitehead and Fort Streets, and Angelea and Catherine Streets
www.florida-keys-vacation.com/BahamaVillage

This is neighborhood marketplace much like visitors would find in the Bahamas, where many of the residents came from. At one time the area wasn't considered safe, especially at night. While night visits are still not recommended, it's become quite a tourist spot during the day. The marketplace covers a lot of territory, with the main entrance being Petronia Street, where a shop inside a house takes center stage. It's Besame Mucho and features beautifully handmade clothing, jewelry, beauty items and gifts. The address of Besame Mucho is 315 Petronia Street, Key West, Florida 33040 and their phone number is 305-294-1928. They are open 10 a.m. to 6 p.m. daily except for Sunday when hours are 10 a.m. to 4 p.m. These are the best times to visit the marketplace and flea market as well. Rows of stalls offer any number of items – beware friendly but prevalent free-roaming chickens as you walk.

Duval Street

Old Town Key West – beginning at Duval and Front Street, Key West, Florida 33040
www.duvalstreet.net

Some of the best and the worst that the city has to offer can be found along Duval Street, which covers many blocks and is a major attraction for tourists interested in shopping or eating.

Highlights include Wyland Studios (for beautiful but fairly expensive sea-themed art), Emeralds International, Crazy Stitch, Earthbound Trading, Key West Aloe for bath and body products, Key West Fabrics (fabrics and clothing), and of course t-shirt and souvenir stores.

Printed in Great Britain
by Amazon.co.uk, Ltd.,
Marston Gate.